For all my dear family and their ebullient
rendition of this song, for Katy in Alaska,
for Nicholas on his island
and for David at home with love

Designed by Joanna Isles
Artwork Production by Bet Ayer
Illustrations copyright © Joanna Isles 1992

For information address:
HYPERION, 114 Fifth Avenue,
New York, New York 10011

Printed and bound in Belgium by Proost

FIRST EDITION
ISBN 1-56282-928-9
10 9 8 7 6 5 4 3 2 1

thank you to Susanne for giving me Folk Hearts -
to Clare and Brian and for Polly's inspiration in
the garden of Casa del Bosco

The
TWELVE
DAYS
OF
Christmas
ILLUSTRATED BY
Joanna Isles

HYPERION

NEW YORK

On the first day
of Christmas
my true love sent to me
A PARTRIDGE
IN A PEAR TREE

On the ·second·
day of Christmas
my true love sent to me
TWO·TURTLE·DOVES
and a partridge
in a pear tree

On the third day
of Christmas
my true love sent to me
THREE FRENCH HENS
two turtle doves
and a partridge
in a pear tree

On the ★fourth★day
of Christmas
my true love sent to me
FOUR·CALLING·BIRDS·
three French hens
two turtle doves
and a partridge
in a pear tree

On the fifth day
of Christmas
my true love sent to me
FIVE · GOLD · RINGS
four calling birds
three French hens
two turtle doves
and a partridge
in a pear tree

On the · sixth · day
of Christmas
my true love sent to me
SIX · GEESE · A · LAYING
five gold rings
four calling birds
three French hens
two turtle doves
and a partridge
in a pear tree

On the seventh day
of Christmas
my true love sent to me
SEVEN·SWANS·A·SWIMMING·
six geese a·laying
five gold rings
four calling birds
three French hens
two turtle doves
and a partridge
in a pear tree

On the eighth day
of Christmas
my true love sent to me
EIGHT MAIDS A·MILKING
seven swans a·swimming
six geese a·laying
five gold rings
four calling birds
three French hens
two turtle doves
and a partridge
in a pear tree

On the *ninth* day
of Christmas
my true love sent to me
NINE*DRUMMERS*DRUMMING
eight maids a-milking
seven swans a-swimming
six geese a-laying
five gold rings
four calling birds
three French hens
two turtle doves
and a partridge
in a pear tree

On the · tenth · day
of Christmas
my true love sent to me
· TEN · PIPERS · PIPING ·
nine drummers drumming
eight maids a·milking
seven swans a·swimming
six geese a·laying
five gold rings
four calling birds
three French hens
two turtle doves
and a partridge
in a pear tree

On the eleventh day
of Christmas
my true love sent to me
ELEVEN·LADIES·DANCING
ten pipers piping
nine drummers drumming
eight maids a·milking
seven swans a·swimming
six geese a·laying
five gold rings
four calling birds
three French hens
two turtle doves
and a partridge
in a pear tree

On the twelfth day
of Christmas
my true love sent to me
TWELVE·LORDS·A·LEAPING
eleven ladies dancing
ten pipers piping
nine drummers drumming
eight maids a·milking
seven swans a·swimming
six geese a·laying
five gold rings
four calling birds
three French hens
two turtle doves
and a partridge
in a pear tree